AF478359

BOOK OF HOPE

O. E. SIMON

Published by
Golden Bell Publishing House Inc.
Box 2680, Grand Forks, B.C. V0H 1H0

ISBN NO. 1-55056-391-2
National and International Copyright 1995
First Edition 1995
Artwork: James Vensel, Marsha Ziska
Photography: J. Simon

Printed in Canada

Dedication

My eager foot stepped on the long since mellowed path of time
And dwelt in regions where the slumb'ring soul seeks rest
While all along the treach'rous ways I did not cease to climb
Then reached the covered hills and struggled onward to the crest
To find the valleys deep beneath for all I searched I left behind.

And here the struggle ended, lost with all the gains of battles won
Amidst a world of envious mortals forging into living space.
I never stepped upon the loser's feeble breath if he was done
Still gave his soul the string which holds to love and life and place
Which from my wife was given unto me to light the rising sun.

And thus this book is dedicated
to my wife, June Simon,
August 28, 1995

A Dedication to the Tower of God

Here amongst the four winds of heaven has faith
carried its seed to fall on the blessed soil of our
country to find its rest and resurrection alike. No
lesser God has caused this piece of forgotten earth
to be selected a shrine of eternal truth than yours
or mine and no lesser faith is unfolded here than
your heart and my heart can ever hope to find but
in an almighty and everlasting God.

Wanderer, should you ever come before this
monument, it was not just coincidence but a destiny
of yours to pass through a millenium of years in only
a few moments that you may freshen your memory. This
country had the enchanted fortune to bless its soil
with the teachings of history, to lend you a smile
of humanity and a golden beam from the sun of Homer.

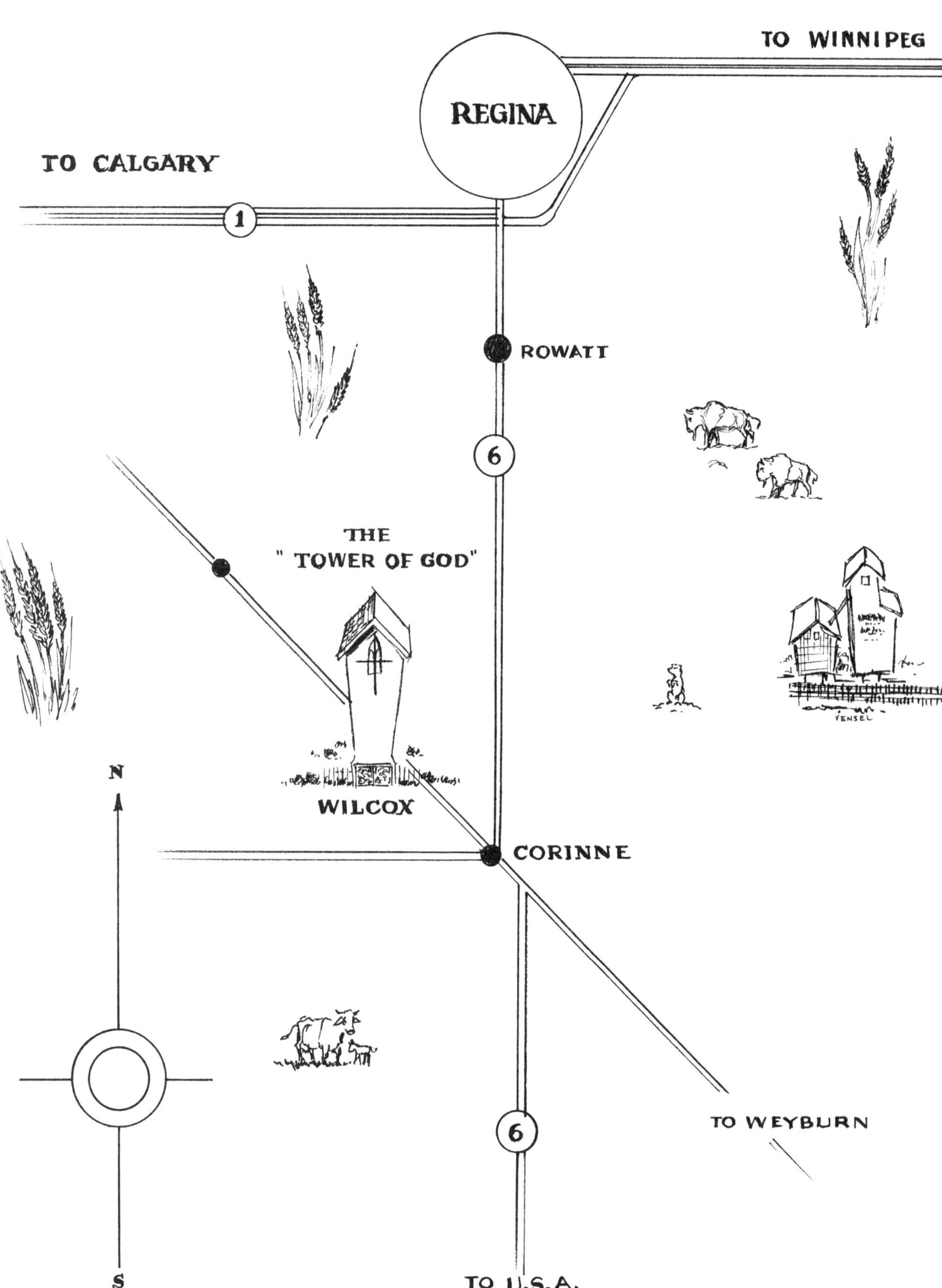

TO WINNIPEG
REGINA
TO CALGARY
1
ROWATT
6
THE
" TOWER OF GOD "
WILCOX
CORINNE
N
S
TO WEYBURN
6
TO U.S.A.
VENSEL

The Tower of God

I found it there in simple beauty waiting
to catch my eye, awake my dreaming soul
to find myself so deeply contemplating
into the past and present, future role,
of man and God and how they are relating.
How easily can then such human goal
of love and understanding bridge the oceans
bring forth to all one holy God's emotions.

The Christian cross shares in the Koran's prayer.
The star of David sanctifying peace
reflects from stones which layer upon layer
still elevate the artifacts from Greece.
Here lives no hostile thought and no betrayer
can hope to spoil nor can he end such lease
which is so beautiful - enshrined in merit
these living thoughts with God's almighty spirit.

And should your road, your destiny, once plan it
that you would like to come, to see and share
into this secret between rocks and granite
your faith and soul, your heart will then declare
to all mankind to say a God had granted
eternal peace to us from everywhere.
Deep from the heart, for all our future giving,
will mankind pray if such a God is living.

VENSEL

The Albatross

The sea ran high, the boat was small,
The elements were growing
And also was the fear of all
In hopeful prayer showing.

It was a day of loud commands
As if all hell was cursing
Four men, one rudder and eight hands
And still the weather wors'ning.

"See there, a ghost, a holocaust!"
The elements abandoned
A fearful cry, high from the mast,
"An Albatross has landed!"

The crew ran fast in utter fear
Like slaves fleeing a Roman.
They ran so fast just to be near
To kill the ghostly omen.

The captain's son, a little child,
Embraced the helpless flyer
And all the men who had been wild
Turned suddenly much shyer.

A beam of light, of sunlight, fell
On to the whirling ocean
And all that had been hell
Now turned to quiet motion.

"Forgive me Dad, it is the bird
I once held in my hand.
When he was small I found him hurt
Tied on his foot this band."

The tall man knelt beside his boy.
He touched his tiny shoulder;
Of all the anger became joy
And old men became older.

If since a stormy ocean was
You'd hear these sailors praying,
Welcoming any Albatross
To an eternal staying.

Faith in Manitou

Wantaneta high on horseback
By the river with her love met
And the morning air felt cool-
When a jealous arrow willing
Struck with evil, silent killing.
From the saddle in the pool
Plunged his lovely body sudden,
Without warning, without sound,
While his horse began to answer
Punishing the stony ground.

Wantaneta saw him falling
By the river and her calling
Of her lover's name was loud:
"Manitou, help with a wonder,
Do not let my love sink under
Whirling waves which are no doubt
Just my tears which seek your justice!"
And she knelt as if to save
Her beloved, wounded warrior,
When his horse jumped in the wave.

And the wave now drew it under,
With more power and more thunder
Burst the overturning surf.
"There's no justice, there's no knowing!"
And she spurred her horse, kept going
Mighty in the river's current,
Fought with clenching, deadly waves,
Fast to pull the wounded lover
From a million twisting graves.

But the faithful warrior's horse found
What was hell or heaven, earthbound,
Pulled his rider on to shore.
No one's seen since Wantaneta
Just her horse came swimming later
Upside down to never more
See the hills and deep green meadows
Where the river passes through-
But the beach has saved in shadows
Lover's faith in Manitou.

In Aeternum

Many times trembled the earth under the mountain's crushing basalt
since temples and pillars have fallen; if not, the victor's torch set
in ruins all beauty that caparisons left for the eye of
history's esteemable watcher. O man, you have little to show
confabulating with Zeus. Your touch is missing Olympus, your
modern times of today owe you still almost a million of sunsets
since Sparta, and sleeping, too distant, rests the Eurotan valley where
Thermoplylae's narrow bound transit has turned into a pasture.
The Periclean Athens deliquesces into the Parthenon's ruins.
In memory let us then travel, setting our foot softly to feel
the broken down marble reflecting Phidias' skill while the
same sun keeps smiling at us rebuilding in thoughts the cradle of art.

> With the songs of age old Sparta
> praising Tyrtaeus still
> slow descending from Mount Ochrys
> wound the column down the hill:
> one more rest before the battle
> seeks the Spartan noble mind
> while a forest out of lances
> leaves the enemy behind.
>
> From the Vales of Tempe marching
> they withdrew from Xerxes' threat
> hundred thousand Medes soldiers
> twenty thousand Hellenes met.
> Now to draw this mighty army
> where the Sperchius River flows,
> there to match where nature warrants
> shield to shields and bow to bows.
>
> And the Pleiads touch the ocean
> and the ocean drinks the sun-
> lost are Thessalies' green valleys
> under such a mighty run.
> Xerxes drives his legion's storm cloud
> dusting like a breeding ghost,
> pouring soldiers, horses, vessels,
> merciless along the coast.

VENSEL

On the shores of Artemiseus
Themistocles sails on guard:
with his fleet of proud tremires
does he break the waves apart.
"Laurium's silver floats for Athens!"
and the Persians fear their sight;
thus, the more, by vengeance pressure
wants their cavalry to fight.

Euribiades, the Spartanian,
led the army for the Greeks
and he met with Themistocles.
Adeimantos thunderous speaks:
"In all games which start too lively
most lose out and do not rise."
In retort said Themistocles,
"But the late one wins no prize."

So deciding their maneuvers
Themistocles sent his slave
to mislead the Mede Mardonius
till the Spartan force was safe
in Thermopylae's narrow canyon
so more hoplites could withdraw,
not to quail, to shield their cities
from the flaming Persian's paw.

VENSEL

Off then marched the Phocian allies
where the track debouches west,
there to stand and back the Spartans
that no Persian climbs the crest.
Well to fortify the heedless
while their shields are turned away
and to give King Leonidas
battleground for his array.

And Mount Callidromus forces
Xerxes' army to the sea
like an ocean which reflected
seeks return in victory.
Bottled, boiled, the brutal war mass
climbing to the narrow spot
where three hundred Spartan warriors
hailed their king and Zeus their god.

 And the road spills Medes warriors
upward into the defile.
"Spartans, long live Lacaedamon!"
while he drew his sword, a smile,
struck the charging Persian phalanx,
"Yes, Leonidas will stand!
Such a king amidst a battle
is a glory to the land!"

Any war is of great evil
and the heros never live
but a king who fights his battle
is a King of Kings to give
moral strength to all his vassals.
With such courage what a peace
could relate the human nations
from this distant land of Greece.

VENSEL

If the quarr'ling politicians
had to combat just themselves
let the people watch the outcome,
there would be no battle hells.
Much too worthwhile is their living
than to die for glory's sake
and withdrawing in its shell is
such a courage's foolish fake.

But when peace is sland'rous threatened
and the cities burn and smoke
and the golden wheatfields flattened-
woe, who dares so to provoke
him, who lived in luscious gardens.
Fiercely turns the righteous man
to protect his homestead wilder
than a hero ever can.

And such hero was this Spartan
raised to fear no conqueror's hoard.
Sanguinary is the harvest
if true courage leads the sword.
Sparks and arrows, crushing helmets,
scimitars torment the air
but the Spartans bold and bolder
did not move from where they were.

While the slain brave Persians' mounting
corpses fell into their rows
shed a shower of insidious
arrows from behind of bows
which a traitor helped to launch.
So, encinctured one by one,
thinned the lines round Leonidas
with the setting of the sun.

VENSEL

And like oil on troubled waters
heaved the battle's mortal waves
while the King stood wildly fighting,
without shield, aside his braves.
Ten more men, one king, still trying
to prevent the time to pass
as a battle ax is cutting
Leonidas to the grass.

There a Persian saw him falling
spurred his horse to final kill
this one king who towered fighting
by his conscience-governed will.
As the charging horse's pasterns
press the life out of his chest,
leaps a blinded Spartan smiling
where the King's sword sounded best.

To the battle's source directing
led his enthusiastic ear.
Everyone around him falling,
no one calling any fear
as his searching arm was touching
Leonidas' ringing sword;
and he died in silent whisper
with a prayer to his Lord.

So it sounded through the ages
from Thermopylae till now,
No one paid these warriors wages
they upheld just their own vow:
"Should, O wanderer, you once pass here
take this sword as message, bring
home to Sparta that we're lying
slain together with our King.

Melt the sword and take its iron,
form a plow to carve the field.
To Apollo's temple carry
Leonidas' rusted shield.
And of us, you tell your children
in all tongues which you may know:
honour is not found in dying
but in hope that peace may grow.

Shalom

(Excerpt from the novel "Shalom")

Forgotten as the moonlit snow, travel
  My thoughts to you, lost destiny,
And heavy rests my breath, my beating heart.
  To you I send my love alone
With such desire to return once more
  Not knowing how I'd envied thee.
My land where freedom scintillates the stars,
  To you, I send this last Shalom.

VENSEL

The Ideal Pleading to Nature

(Excerpt from the play "Decay of the Soul")

Welcome to you, eternal sun. Your light
flows through my soul so warm and always
smiling have you begun these times since I
recall - regardless whether night or day,
no destiny refused your blessing touch.
Again I give, returning all your splendour,
my thoughts to living spirits as I speak
of Nature's pleasant forms: the way my eye
enriches you, O soul, greeting the flowing
river in the valley, so distant but
so close is life and light united,
keep passing with your golden beams across
toward ancient and the present temples.

One god endured along the treacherous paths
of destiny which man created out
of greed and ignorance, of jealousy,
to turn the evil forces on to me.

And now, your light, your sunbeam warms my gown
to lift the veils which Demeter has laid -
forth cometh the dark green field - on Mount Olymp
is opening the cloud which covered time,
dark ages, the betrayal of man himself.
If just the mind could read the eye's impressions
while they profoundly are engaged in drinking
of all that has been spilled in beauty mild
or hold the harshness of the laws to end,
to overcome, outlast, outgrow, all ways,
all evil thoughts would be reflected fast
and warned to well protect what generations
spent in painful efforts to establish.

YENSEL

…Would king and peasant multiply the treasures
which grew out of the breathing soul,
reincarnate the minds to evermore
paint, build, sing, write and speak of thee,
thou Sun, who touches without prejudice:
complete what time has left to form in every
stone and bubbling spring to bless your light,
inspire one more day the sculptor's hand
so that he may create a monument
worthy of thee to capture all your light.
If darker ages should again refuse
my faith to influence the spirit of the blessed;
My hope, thou light, endure more centuries,
mature with every sunrise to overcome
the cold and awesome cycles, to preserve,
to teach, what I have learned that betterment,
in part, rests in man's chest and the desire
to be true is born in him and nourished
through experience and through hardship often.
Not always just by reason emerged the
mind which echoes through the space of time:
it was that well spilled fortune which unites
the harsh so cleverly with Nature's soft
alloys, that like the mantle of a bell
composeth such a reaching sound that ear
and heart combined, may cause the tear to flow.
And still I speak of distant ages. Time
has judged and clearly kept defined that truth
may lose its silky veil and drift along
till false ambition will arouse the friend.
The hand which orderly directs the plow
now draws the sword and stirs the burning oil
while unaware of me who shaded him with peace.

VENSEL

Regardless of your will I would remain
and wait, if just one soul, one searching mind,
if just one spirit needed me to live.
I would not fail my ancient gods to save
one man who cared for faith and not for gold -
and, if my conscience showed a shadow now
man has no future, had no glorious past.

This is man's final step onto a stage
where you reside since time began to count
the start of all beginning in your light.
Is this your cycle, Nature, now to end
in tempting man to further challenge you,
let him control what you controlled, what you
in many ways have mastered perfectly
in order to prepare his death, that man
must live a new, more pure and more refined,
clean life, all from the very start of time
and try to teach him what the past has failed
to teach? O Nature, you surrounded him
gave of your treasures rich and plentiful
and so distracted he forgot to think,
to learn to master you within himself.

VENSEL

Glow then your golden flow of light.
Life without end sink into night and fill
the moonlit world to dream around in peace.
Kiss all the silent planets and the stars,
pour out your treasures to be seen and felt
and millions will escape the awesome dark
which lingers in the judgement hour.

Alike the color of my gown, snow white,
is my intention still. I always gave my best,
myself, with soul and heart and now in front
of you I wait. No sign has come to me
that I could see or sense that I am wanted.
If desolate I must remain with all
my hope another spirit in myself
may grant me patience so my thoughts may rest
to greet you one more time, O loving light,
that you may calm my frightened mind.
Last hope, let us persuade the world to change.
In one more final try shall destiny
become my friend before this world will end
if you withdraw your light from me.

VENSEL

The Golden Bell

Careful in the early morning
Faded what the night had held
All the shadows into sunshine
From the heaven to be felt.
Then the chapel's bell rang warning
To recess from trade and art
To kneel down to bless the power
Which the sunlight gave its start.

Wonders, wonders without ending
Rang the bell deep in the hearts
May all live, may no one perish
Spoke reflecting golden darts
From the bell the sun was sending.
Then the story was retold
That in fact such beauty sounding
Only could ring out of gold.

As two greedy looking faces
Watched the sunbeam's pleasing game
Dancing, meditative spirits
Which the bell tried to proclaim
While temptation now embraces
What their evil thoughts have planned,
Kissed the sunlight much more pensive
As the bell had blessed the land.

VENSEL

Using now the silent hour
They pretend to pray inside
Leaving no suspicion spoiling
What their eyes held still in sight
To climb up into the tower
And to steal from, all the gold,
Chip away the costly mineral
Filling all their bag could hold.

Noontime came from Zenith, greeting,
High stood now the smiling sun
When the two faced all the riches
Saw the wealth which was to come
Somehow from this dev'lish meeting.
And to muffle the first blow
They wrapped cloth around the centre
Where the bell curved like a bow.

And they tried to carve and hammer
Metal from the shiny bell
Hard and harder wore the surface
To resist and like a spell
Lost the shiny bell its glamour
And the thieves for all they knew,
"How could gold turn into iron?"
Then the fear inside them grew!

Fast to leave the morbid tower
Where such miracles were near
in bright daylight, blue sky'd heaven,
How could gold then disappear?
Who holds such a giant power
to unveil a scheming plot:
Only one who is almighty
And who has the touch of God.

The two thieves went to the Father
And they told him of their try
How the bell turned into iron
As they both were standing by.
And they felt the silence bother
But they could not tell him why
Such a change could really happen
When the Father passed them by.

And he went to get two crosses
And they were of real gold,
Gave them to the two men waiting:
"This is for you to behold.
Loss amongst the greatest losses
Is the conscience that you've kept
In your penance brothers sleeping
Rest the tears which I have wept."

Four White Cranes

I have seen one summer morning
 Early when the dew still slept
  Just before the sun's rays warming
   Crystals dreaming, grass stems kept
     Four white cranes enshrined in pleasure
      Borrowed from the goddess' treasure
        Like a sweet delirium.

I have watched this summer morning
 When the wind forgot to breathe
  How without a single warning
   Just for me as if to please
     All the cranes, the four together,
      Rose into the air to ever
        Hail my own Elysium.

The One From Avalon

The torch was bright, the night reflecting
What once the veil of darkness hid
And in pursuit he was neglecting
To wear the shield aside his hip,
To guard himself where lurking traitors
May find a spot, and Heaven knows
If miracles and wonders, craters
Obscure his path with friends or foes.
And with the wind his horse suspending
Was all his love and fortune lending.

To save his friend he was returning
Away from battlefield and fame.
The Knight from Avalon was earning
An unjust, horrifying name.
His left clenched to the torchlight solid
His right hand on the rein,
Above his heart he wore the wallet
With all the evidence to gain -
One hour's time to save the city
And not one second for his pity.

From Avalon, its rising towers,
Here all the guards withdrawn tonight
A distant battle steals the powers,
A false attack before the fight.
O scheming mind, what treach'rous smiling
Inherited the other sword?
How adds up lie on lie compiling
A melody with such discord?
The one from Avalon was coming
Like time and faith in shadows running.

The drawbridge falls into the silence
A ghostly rider leaves the town
A sleeping battle senses vi'lence
Before the wounded falleth down.
He chose, this knight, for his protection
The colours of the traitor's side
He was the cross of resurrection
And cov'ring was the decoyed hide
The mark by which his friends would know him
Inside the walls or outside going.

VENSEL

The one from Avalon was aiming
In full gallop down from the hill
Fast on the ghostly rider, gaining
Short'ning the distance for the kill.
There was no cross, no mark of brothers,
There was no sign of trust around.
"A traitor just like all the others!"
His thrusting sword came wild and found
The centre full, a sinking shadow
Fell backwards on the dew-touched meadow.

Again the torch is shooting higher,
Like liberated from the draft,
The steaming horse, mixed with such fire,
Made war, such war, a cruel craft.
If seconds can divide the Heaven
Oh what a force will soon become
Springs of one hour if once given
We kill the father or the son
We find no time to hear the other
To save a friend we kill our brother.

The Knight from Avalon not knowing
Turned on the spot away from here
Again his horse's hoofs were going
Until the city's walls were near.
"We are betrayed, here is the paper!"
He pulled his wallet with all might
While an eternal moment later
A stray gone arrow struck his side.
The one from Avalon was dying
And brother close to brother lying.

Now in the face of love and error
Of duty and of loyalty,
If hist'ry looks in its mirror
It talks of hero's royalty.
The sword which draws a bleeding geyser
Compare once to a planting hand,
Behold and pray that you get wiser
To turn the fire from your land.
Then, in the face of God and duty,
Where find I love to find some beauty.

The Hexameter

Phosphorous, bringer of promising light, why are you hiding from us
now, when the mornings rise slower with hope in exegetical shadows?
Had I not seen your past years I never would notice just
how you deceive us, refusing the light, morning's warm welcome,
rivers' keen rapids. But peace left the pastures, cruelly are raging the wars.
Centuries hurry to bypass the time and wonder that life still exists
amidst the pitiable cities in ills that flesh seeks, despising their gods,
heresy losing itself till the heaven will fall. Where were you son of
bright flowing lights? Cerberes waiting called back you to darkness?
Or yet was it a dream dreamt by gods, heavenly, showing your star,
spending such glow that, like climbing veils, mist embracingly gathered
the shapely curves on wakening hills and Aphrodite, lover of
Joy, yet the queen of smiles, crowned you Hesperus once?
Ate was watching with fullest intent: hate forming dark clouds drawn
over Elysium's mild growing gardens. It changed what was trust.
Protection was offered to swindle and lie and lost was the stallion's
sun-glowing wings who once set the mood of Zephirus greeting his isle.
Filled is the earth since with desolate pain. Man has still not learned that
hist'ry repeats all its glorious temptations between sunshine and rain.
Glowing in lightning is soaring a flame unduly earned in shame.
Suffers the decently worshipping man asking for God to return.
Always again this God, not hesitating, lovingly pleasing,
hails us and sunlight returns downward in splendour flooding with love,
with such caring, life-spending flow that ruins of Athens grow tall
in this beautiful white that more cleaner the eye's cherishing hope
rests on the landscape and you colourful Nature never left us.
Over the treetops the high sailing eagle's wing touches the sun
and his shadow strives close and it vibrates the peaceloving grass.
This is the place where Aeoshylos worships. Not such a spot
dwindled through history's times and not such a day can be obtained
without that we shiver if fast flashing lightning thunders destruction,
frightens the valley from heaven to earth not touching the temples.
And here is where hope has buried its treasure in the peaceloving soul
deeply combined with the pleasures of seeing a night or a day
be it a sunbeam, a shooting star's tail - if not engraved stays the sky.
The soul of a child will count wonders with innocence still.

A Day Which Never May Arrive

A day which never may arrive
is if they separate this land
and draw a border between wife,
her husband or her child,
refuse a brother's helping hand
yet hoping to survive.

I could not bear my son to aim
his sights against a brother's chest:
the glory that was Quebec's name
will lose in history
and all of Canada would rest
in pity and in shame.

But should such day once overcome
what generations built with pride:
a border's separating run
divides this Canada
I would not live on either side
and wish I had no son.

About the Author:

Being the product of a Europe in war, the author saw both man at his best and at his worst. After surviving the prison camps and the post-war agonies, though educated in Germany, receiving a National literary prize for his Dornberger Hexameter, the author decided to seek out a new country where he could work, dream and hope to be a part of a new and better future for mankind.

Now internationally known, he remains a citizen of Canada living in seclusion, still travelling, writing, teaching the philosophy he has ascribed to for most of his life.

The Quadriga is a set of four volumes of poetry. The first, "The Book of Thought," was originally published in 1972 under the author's preudonym, Falo Nomis. It speaks of his love for his new home and his observations of the world of man. "The Book of Hope" was inspired by the late Canadian extraordinaire, Monseigneur Athol Murray, as it is dedicated to his "Tower of God" found at the Notre Dame University just south of Regina in Wilcox, Saskatchewan.

"The Book of Life" and "The Book of Destiny" will be published within the next two years.

Other Books by O.E. Simon:

Shalom - a fictional novel about
the life of Anya Ulyaev, a
Russian doctor in the prison
camps of Siberia, and her
struggle to save the life of
an Allied prisoner

Curse of the Gods - a spy novel
about conditions in Germany
after World War II

Book of Thought - a book of
poetry, forming part of the
Quadriga